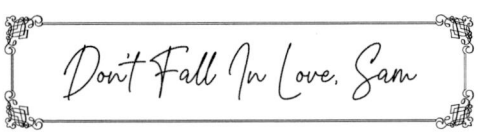

DON'T FALL IN LOVE, SAM
Author: Sam Morris
2020

Layout & design by Sexy*design* studio / @sexydesing.studio
Edit & synopsis by Cole Collins

Published by Sam Morris
Sam Morris ©
www.sammorris.me

Content copyright © Sam Morris, 2020
Illustrations copyright © Sam Morris, 2020

All rights reserved.

No portion of this book may be reproduced, stored in a retrieval system transmitted at any time or by any means mechanical, electronic, photocopying, recording or otherwise, without the prior, written permission of the publisher.

The right of Sam Morris to be identified as the author of this work has been asserted by him in accordance with the Copyright, Designs and Patents act 1988.

Names have been changed in this book to protect the identity of individuals.

ISBN 9781800491441

*For Javier, Luis, Marcel, & Shelby.
And of course, Berlin.*

Foreword 8
Ghosted 14
~~Beautiful~~ 22
Flaws 28
~~Pride~~ 32
Things That Cause Me Anxiety 34
Doing My Best 38
Barcelona 42
Closure? 48
Departure 52
Unclear Intentions 54
The 8 Instructions 62
Don't Fall In Love, Sam 72
Copenhagen Boy 82
Some Days 86

~~Cheating~~ 90
Lucky Escape 94
~~Fearless~~ 96
~~Existing~~ 98
Love is 104
That's Not Me 108
Fiction 112
A Friend In Him 118
Untitled 120
A Fig Leaf 122
Winter 130
I Didn't Say No 134
Mine 158
Circle Of Stones 162

Foreword

The constant change of pace. The drama in the unforeseen. The excitement in the fear of change. This is the way I have always approached life. I try not to plan ahead and I always like to keep things fresh. A rolling stone gathers no moss. I've had a very colourful life, from a young age, I guess it's made me hungry for the different and exciting. It's made me steer away from the mundane and sensible. I've always had a love for writing: poetry, stories, songwriting. It's been a way to express myself, to vent, to escape. I'd always written out my fears and calamities, my heartaches and crushes. My dreams have always been muddled. I never understood the concept of the 5-year goal, and I certainly didn't want to learn about it or adhere to it. I take every day as an opportunity to create something. A footprint to leave behind. Whilst I was learning about myself as a gay man during my late teens and early twenties, I would feed on my favourite films, books, TV shows, music, until I should've been full. Nothing was ever enough. Including my first loves. I would love them with all my might, so much so, it was like showing love to a butterfly by grasping it in a closed fist.

Everything was fleeting, and my life became a series of misadventures that led me to a life, which many questioned how I arrived to be at. I skipped from one vocation to the next, never really settling my feet on the ground. I traveled to run, and I ran to learn. I was insecure, and I subject myself to imposter syndrome in whichever craft I turned my hand to. I knew I had natural talents, but I wasn't sure which outlet would finally be mine. My life had been changing quite quickly before I left London. I'd been travelling so much and had never been in one place for too long. It was Berlin that finally stole my heart. It's a city perfect for my type. The introvert with a love for a similar people. Underground art, outlier parties, and liberation in queerness. It was like being given a key to a utopia I didn't know existed, at first, then I realised, behind any bright figure, hides a shadow. This isn't to suggest that Berlin has a sinister side unlike anywhere else. Many places have pros and cons, but I had never really been around anywhere long enough to face them. Apart from London. Its nonchalant approach to the erasure of queer culture was one of the reasons I left. Nearly every gay bar or club in London had closed down around me in the course of a decade. It was too disappointing to stick around.

So, I had gone to Berlin to feel something again. To taste, smell, and feel life. Queer life. Embrace sex, love, and nudity. And I felt it, I felt it hard. The good, the bad, and the ugly. I had always been writing about my experiences before my move to Berlin, and I continued more thoroughly after my move. I journaled everything that made an impact, or that provoked a certain thought within me. When I looked back at these 4 years of stories, I felt like I was reading the struggles and experiences of not just my queer experience, but probably the experiences of many. I looked at myself in these situations like an outsider. I laughed with him, I cried with him, and at times I felt a deep frustration for him. I thought it would be exposing to share these stories with the world, but important to give these moments a voice, to show they existed. I decided to put them all into a book, but it needed to mirror my life. Fast paced, ever changing, and fortuitous. It needed to be an accurate representation of my truth in those years, and so it was inevitable that the genre of the book would have to take the reader on a rollercoaster. I experienced highs and lows in these years, not all in Berlin, sometimes on my travels. Some things challenged my humanity and self-worth, and I often used music and poetry in many of these times, so I felt it necessary to keep these moments in between the stories of the book.

I learned a lot about sex, love, hate, empowerment, and drive, and I wanted to pass on these lessons to those who end up with this book in their hands. Being a young adult gay man is like constantly being in adolescence, extremes are irrational, and feelings are fleeting. We learn about love and relations on our own personal journeys, by taking the jigsaw pieces of heterosexual people, and bending them to fit our atypical picture.

In this book of stories, I take you on my own personal journey over the course of a few years. Sometimes it's funny, sexy, or naughty, but sometimes it's dark, sad, and haunting, and that's a truthful reality of a (gay) person navigating their way through this world as an adult.

I hope this collection of events inspires those reading to find a stronger sense of self, find the strength to overcome darkness and most importantly, learn to believe in love again, for yourself and for others.

Ghosted

"Don't fall in love, Sam."

That's what a guy once said to me as I was laying on top of him naked and we were in the middle of having sex staring into each other's eyes.

"Don't fall in love, Sam."

I wasn't sure why it hurt so much when he said it. I wasn't really looking for a relationship, at all, but it was like a knife slowly sliding into my heart. I'd been pretty emotionally vulnerable since I moved to Berlin and it seemed like I was having a string of sort-of-relationships one after the other, like a multiple vehicle collision.

This boy was an Italian student visiting Berlin and I let him stay with me for a few days. He lived in Copenhagen and so the logistics of having a relationship with him looked unlikely, which made the whole thing super attractive to me, because as my therapist had told me: I seem to be excited by impossibility.

I like to collect red flags and fashion them into beautiful scarves.

During one of our sessions, while I was in the middle of this unrequited relationship, my therapist asked, 'Why him?' I replied, 'I don't know.' She continued to interrogate me, asking 'Why are you going to Copenhagen? Why him?'

I really didn't have an answer.

This therapist was a little bit out of the ordinary, anyway. She was very direct, super Freudian; I lay down on the couch, while she sat in silence and scribbled things, looking at me with contempt, occasionally glancing down at her watch, waiting for me to take a breath in the middle of an emotional breakthrough, so she could whisper, 'Ohhh-kay that's time up for today'.

I started seeing a therapist after pressure from friends who were, quite frankly, tired of my daily stresses. I have really bad health anxiety, which didn't really improve after moving to Berlin. I've never had gonorrhoea so many times in one period. I couldn't even think about getting a blow job without being prescribed a course of Azithromycin.

I worry about all sorts of diseases, on a daily basis. I'm convinced I have some sort of cancer almost every week, and if I even feel a slight twinge somewhere in my body my fingers are all over that shit like I'm kneading dough. I can spend hours looking for a lump. So much so, that I end up bruised; the pain from that subsequently charges up my health anxiety again. It's a never-ending circle of fretting.

It is exhausting. But who isn't exhausted by their anxieties in 2020. I think at this point it's just a race to the end now, and if you get through it without the need for a therapist, before climate change kills us all, then you deserve a gold medal.

So after taking the advice of my friends, attempting to make sense of why I felt the ways I did, and after seeing my therapist a few times, I decided she wasn't right for me. And in a weird twist of events, I ended up being her therapist.

One day I turned up for my usual session at 5pm, and I rang the doorbell. No answer. So, I rang again, and still got no response. I thought this was a bit weird, so I decided to give her a call. She didn't answer, so I gave up and went home – I was a bit pissed off to be honest. I texted her, to which she replied that I'd got the time wrong. I was 99% certain I hadn't.

Still confused, I decided to rearrange the appointment. But still she was being distant and weird; not replying to my messages for days. I thought 'of course, I'm being ghosted by my fucking therapist'. Eventually, she stopped replying to my text messages and emails – I had been officially, emotionally abandoned by my therapist. I worried, if she can't handle me, what chance do I have?

Two weeks later she emailed me with an explanation.

She had had a fake client arrive to her house for a session, he had knocked her unconscious and stole everything in her apartment, including her phones and laptops.

I was in shock. I'd heard some crazy excuses from guys not wanting a second date, but this was an absolutely wild story, if it was just an excuse not to see me again. She asked if I wanted to arrange a new appointment, but I felt like now the energy was all off, and it seemed like she needed the care more than me. She'd explained this harrowing series of events that had taken place, and then asked me if I wanted to schedule a new session. I didn't really know what to say, honestly, I obviously hoped she was OK, both physically and psychologically; but I couldn't really imagine moving forward, sitting opposite this beaten up woman, telling her my problems. However, I did eventually go back. I returned to a frail lady with 2 black eyes, although she said she was recovering well. That being said sitting with her in that session, trying to talk about myself and my woes to a robbery victim just felt weird. I spent the first 15 minutes of our session asking her how she was, which was an odd shift in the power dynamic. And then I felt like all of my issues seemed superficial in light of her recent experience, and actually I felt uncomfortable sitting across from her black and blue face talking about my boy problems.

So, I quit. I quit therapy.

I went back to my notebook and I started writing everything down.

Beautiful

I've never really felt beautiful. I think the last time I truly ever believed that I was beautiful was when I was 12 years old. It was a picture of me smiling – happy – before I started puberty. The innocence of youth beaming from my face. I think I looked pretty. From there it seemed to go downhill, and rapidly. I developed late as a teenager, and while I didn't really get the usual teenage acne, I did develop this seemingly gormless appearance. I suddenly had a huge nose, a sprouting chin, and an aggressively protruding Adam's apple. I used to sit on the train every day on the way to school, looking at my side reflection in the window, internalising a building hatred for the way I looked. I used to think I was disgusting. I remember thinking I looked like a wicked witch, caricatured in the pages of a children's story. I would focus in on my flaws, beating myself up with them, it depleted any confidence I had left by the time I got to school.

At school I was an outlier. I didn't have a lot of friends, only a few close ones. I was usually in my own world, taking in the environment, and observing people's behaviours. I've always found people very odd; the way they communicate, and socialise, all trying to please one another so as to make themselves feel/look better. I never wanted to be a part of this, but I used to envy their confidence. I discovered I was gay around the age of 16, and it was another heavy burden weighing on my mind. I remember thinking, why do I have to deal with this as well as everything else?

I was newly finding my sexuality after I started college, and I didn't know how to tell my first crush that I liked him. I remember finding his number through a friend, and texting him, telling him how I felt. He ended up telling everyone at the school. I never really thought that I'd ever find a boyfriend because I perceived gay men's confidence to only be found in physical beauty, a sort of beauty seen on the front cover of a magazine, or in movies, which I certainly felt I didn't belong. Until one day. I was approached by a guy who was doing the lighting for one of our college shows. He was so beautiful, classically handsome, and lots of people at the school had a crush on him. I had been shyly looking at him for a few days, but never thought in a million years he would be interested in me. He came up to me one afternoon, gave me his card, and told me to message him and that we should go for a drink. I remember physically falling down the stairs, turning around and running to my friends to tell them the news. I was elated, but also confused – somehow, I felt it wasn't real. He ended up being my first lover. It wasn't love, but it was my first sexual and intimate experience with another man, and it was very special.

I've had 3 serious gay relationships since then. I've broken my heart a few times over, and with each relationship it seems to get more painful.

I have reached a point in my life where I've found love for myself. I feel proud of my sexuality wholeheartedly, and, if anything, I want to be a beacon of hope to any young gay men who may not fully love themselves.

My self-image is something I'm still trying to learn to love. I have found a way to make myself look beautiful, through the art of photography and film. I know which angles will celebrate my body rather than shame it. Does this mean I'm confident in my beauty? No. Does it mean I've reached a point of contentment in the way that I look? Almost. The demons that enter your life in your formative years often stay for a good while. It's taken me a long time to accept the shell that I'm in, but I hope that I'm finally getting there.

Flaws

These flaws I call my own.
I recognise and often moan,
but never would I disown
the things that always make me groan.
My fingers serve me well
and I see the tree from which I fell,
the poems on my hands to tell
the stories of a little girl.
The smells on us we wash away
but some they linger in our brains,
of people, things, and lonely days.
The naked smell is one that stays.
My nose, my biggest enemy,
so hated by the rest of me
but loved for it's intensity

of choosing what is best for me.
The hair it spares the thoughts of those
who linger by the feet and toes
ignoring flaws of yester-woes
and deliver so the ebbs and flows.
The little freckles, spots & moles,
join the dots of stories told
and within the darkness of the folds
are bronzes, browns and rose golds.
The extremities did feel the storm,
tore, and cracked, the rose and thorn.
The broken lovers I will mourn,
who gave it up to be reborn.
Lines and greys, we wish away
but I will welcome them to stay.
The things that I have heard and seen
will live upon my head and gleam.
Embrace the drips, the reds and pinks,
the jagged, spots, and twisted kinks.
The holes, the skin, the parts that stink,
the big, the small, the overthink.
The marks, the tits, the mind, the guts,
the massive, and the tiny butts,
the hidden, and the surface cuts,

the yellow teeth, and ugly nuts.
Just love yourself. You're enough.
The love you give need not be tough.
Just love yourself, it's just above,
the amount you think, is just enough.

Pride

$\mathcal{I}'m$ in London on the tube with ripped jeans and a sheer red leotard top with sequins, I can feel the eyes all over me. Darting, examining, eyes. Eyes to observe and experience. Eyes who are unfamiliar and interested. I can feel them questioning, but I can also feel their gentle intrigue. All harsh judgment comes with intrigue. And today, it's London Pride, I can feel it. While many walks of life loiter around the city, eyes are still a wander. The normal day is disrupted and the ordinary are thrown out of their comfort zone. Like an old-fashioned freak show, they should be charged ticket admission for the way they look at you. Instead, I stand proudly among their glares. I stand.

I stand and think, it's time to move to Berlin●

Things That Cause Me Anxiety

- » HIV and AIDS

- » Skin cancer, from moles or freckles

- » That my PrEP won't work & I'll contract HIV

- » That I'll have anal cancer cause by undiagnosed HPV

- » Oral/Throat cancer caused by undiagnosed HPV

- » Hepatitis, always looking for pain in back from liver

- » Yellow skin and eyes

- » Kidney infection

- » Testicular cancer, lumps on balls

- » Bowel cancer from bad diet, belly aches

- » Ongoing fear of appendicitis

- » Veins in legs, varicose, DVT, blood clots

- » Antibiotic resistance from STDs

- » Teeth problems, decay, ulcers, gum disease

- » Scalp issues, dandruff, psoriasis

- » Lower back crunching, spinal issues

- » Sensitive skin patches, caused by unknown illness/nerve damage

- » Syphilis chancres, or not knowing I'm already stage 2/3 and getting brain damage

Doing My Best

I knew it was going to make me sick. With every sip, I thought about my health and the following day. The risk didn't outweigh the torment of the anxiety I would feel turning up to a house party full of strangers for pre-drinks. I drank so I could become someone else. Someone who wasn't scared of people, who felt different. When I'm around new people, particularly in an intimate setting like a stranger's apartment, feeling alienated in someone else's space, I feel completely and utterly out of my comfort zone. I think I'm worthless and ugly; I imagine that people will wonder why I'm even there. I try harder to seem polite, in fear of people thinking I'm arrogant, and I work harder in conversation to seem more interesting. Drink loosens this whole process up a bit. It makes it feel less difficult. I think they'll prefer the drunk me to the sober me, full to the brim with anxiety. I never had huge groups of friends growing up. Always just one or two. I moved schools quite a lot, and so at each school I would find just one person I could connect with. I would give them all my energy, and then I felt safe. This has followed me through life, and I find big groups of people overwhelming and difficult to navigate. I revert into my shell, and feel insanely self-conscious and unworthy. Even being around people in a group of more than 3 or 4 gives me enough anxiety to send me into a depressive episode. I try my hardest to overcome these feelings, usually it's ok in small doses, as long as I have a good amount of personal time in between to reboot.

Living in foreign cities it helps, just to make friends. But I know within that group there's someone there who doesn't warm to me, and that feeling outweighs everything else – I just want out. That's why I end up battling with loneliness; it's a friend and an enemy. Sometimes it saves me from the horrible situations of being stuck in a room full of people who I practically feel phobic of; other times it locks me away, alone, and makes me feel unloveable. Either way, each scenario makes me feel unloveable. It's sad. It hurts. It's inescapable. It's unbearable. This is why I find my escape through art, and photography, and social media. It's a way to connect to people, while staying in my comfort zone. I don't want every day to feel like I'm queuing up for a ride at a theme park. The mix of anxiety, anticipation, nausea, it's not a sustainable way of living life. I want my life to be easy, and I haven't yet deciphered the code that will allow me to manage that. Yet●

Barcelona

After arriving in Barcelona, to my beautiful apartment in Eixample, I was excited. Excited to see the city, visit the beach, taste the food, but mainly, taste the men. After a few days at my new place, a cute local boy offered to come over and make me food. He introduced me to gazpacho, and after the first few mouthfuls, I grew to like this cold, tomato juice, soup. As we were cleaning up the kitchen my Airbnb host came home. She had seemed very cool, we had spent some time together the first few nights, and so I had no qualms about bringing somebody over. She decided to go to bed early and my new local friend and I decided to watch a movie, then he grabbed his motorbike helmet and went home around 11pm.

The following day I got up and went for coffee. After going out and grabbing my sweet milk coffee, I got a WhatsApp message from my Airbnb host telling me that I cannot have guests over whatsoever. She apologised that she didn't make it clear when advertising the place, but said that I was welcome to find somewhere else to stay if it was an inconvenience. I was a little pissed, but I wasn't about to make myself homeless and start looking for somewhere else to live, so I apologised and said it wouldn't happen again.

A few weeks had passed, and my trip in Barcelona was nearing it's end. It was a hot Friday afternoon, and while sat at home, alone, feeling horny, I opened the old faithful, Grindr. My Airbnb host worked full time, so that day I was home alone and feeling like the world was my oyster. There was a guy online who I'd hooked up with a few weeks earlier: he was available and horny. He told me he hadn't shot his load for about 5 days, and that had me at full mast. He was only around the corner, and I said I could host. He could be there in 10mins, but it was more like 5. I left the door open and waited on the bed for him, naked. He got undressed in the hall, and walked in, also naked. He had a beautiful dick. He walked over to me and put it in my mouth. His dick was the perfect size; husband dick, the kind you could take every night. I wasn't in the mood for anal, but he turned me onto my front and ate me out anyway. It got him super horny, and it wasn't long before he turned me back around, and as I was sucking his throbbing uncut dick, he pulled his dick out of my mouth, arched up, and blew his load all over my face. He stepped back, out of breath, and asked if he could use the bathroom. I nodded and pointed to the hall. As he went to the bathroom, I finished myself off.

In the meantime, he had put most of his clothes back on and walked back into my room to get his watch. As I was wiping his cum off my face, I heard the front door creak open and my Airbnb host shout 'hello?!' I ran to my bedroom door, slammed it shut and locked the inside bolt, all the while running around the room with cum dripping off my face, manically saying, 'Oh my God!', over and over again. I was trying to work out what the fuck I was going to do. I turned around to see the boy I had just blown, sitting on my bed, his face frozen in horror, adding to the hilarity of the situation. We were both now locked in my bedroom, panicking; his shoes, jacket, and bag were all in the hall for my host to see.

I was trying to come up with a million different excuses to get me out of this mess. I was now getting panic dressed, in front of this boy, who barely spoke English, while he was asking me questions, nervously pacing around my room. I kept saying to him that it was fine, and that I would just say that he was a friend of mine; that we were just popping back home to pick something up before going out again. It was at that point I leant forward and said, 'What's your name?'. I had no fucking idea what his name was. I waited for the apartment to go quiet, which would hopefully mean she'd disappeared into her room.

Then we could make our escape. We were ready. Waiting. I told him to just grab his stuff from the hall, and we would both leave together. I opened the bedroom door and we made a run for it. I opened the front door, bolted in to the stairwell and he finished getting dressed. 'You are a disaster,' he said to me in a thick Spanish accent, shaking his head. I was laughing so hard by this point I had tears running down my face. As we left the building, before we said goodbye, I asked him if I had any cum left on my face. He giggled and shook his head. I had dried cum-tissue all over my hand, which I spent the walk to a nearby coffee shop trying to pick off, bit by bit. In hindsight it occurred to me that the boy didn't know who had actually come home. Maybe the reason he looked so panicked was because he thought it was my husband, or worse, wife, and he was about to be an unexpected guest star in a real life telenovela.

Poor Sergio. If you're reading this, thank you, for a great facial, and a very funny afternoon.

Closure?

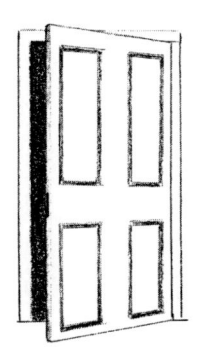

$\mathcal{A}s$ I looked down at his face straining to squeeze all of my limp cock into his mouth, I knew it was over.

I'd been seeing my ex on and off for a while. We'd go for dinner and hang out; it was always really sweet, same as always, tactile and loving. We enjoyed the same conversations, with an amnesia of the issues we had faced before. Nostalgic. We hadn't had sex for over two years, so the ultimate test of our relationship surviving a reprise would be to see if the sex was still alive. We used to have the most amazingly passionate sex. He's pretty hung and he would fuck me really deep. We connected chemically and our scents intertwined to create a frenzy of senses. Our sex was wild. We would roll around for hours covered in oil, fucking over and over again. Dionysian. It was mind blowing, and a time when we would forget about all our other issues, so I could always count on time in the bedroom to save the day.

However, the reprise was not as it had been. Our connection was off. Kissing him felt different, almost as if we couldn't get in sync, and every time I looked into his eyes, as he was fucking me, I saw the crying, desperate mess that he used to be on FaceTime while we dated. The bedroom no longer made our problems disappear. As he sucked my dick, I looked at his face and felt a feeling of deep sadness and pity. I immediately lost my hard-on. I urged him to just fuck me. I turned over. I couldn't look at his face. He was still hard, and it would let me escape the mortification of what had just happened. We fucked, but the spark and passion was gone, drowned out by the sound of the bed creaking like crazy.

The next morning, we had coffee together, exchanged pleasantries, and he left. As he kissed me on the lips to say goodbye, and I closed the door, I found peace in knowing that it was over. After three years of non-stop drama, of extremely dark thoughts of sadness, of feelings of love, heartache and pure passion, it was finally over. I was ready and able to finally walk away from something that had changed my life forever. I had been given the signs that I needed. I finally understood what closure meant. That feeling of inner calm is undeniable: it's apparent, there, palpable. I was free, finally●

Departure

Night my love,
I'll see you in the dark,
Wishing for the morning
And the strangers in the park.
I know it's just for now
And not tomorrow with a story.
I leave with you a scent
While we walk a separate journey.
The wetness of your skin,
Reflecting in the blues and reds
And our juices overflowing
As we rest upon our heads.
I loved you for a moment,
Just a flicker of a light.
A kiss I'll leave for you,
As you depart into the night.

Unclear Intentions

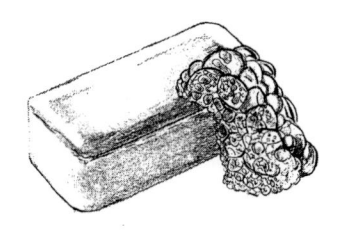

$\mathcal{I}t$ started off as a bit of fun. I thought it was a quirk, not knowing it signalled a red flag. He would pull down my trousers, then my underwear, then mockingly inspect my dick. He would pull back my foreskin, bring his nose very close to my dick, and would let me know if it smelt. I found it humiliating and uncomfortable, but I laughed it off. I think before you've had sex with someone, to be analysed in such a de-sexualising way is pretty bizarre. I found it super uncomfortable but tried to not let it bother me too much. I wasn't quite sure how to address it at first, so I left it. He had told me that I need to wear my foreskin back all the time in my underwear so that my dick doesn't smell, like dick. I know my dick is clean. I had never encountered a guy with this sort of obsessive approach to male cleanliness, but I wasn't a fan. I personally quite like smells. A slightly musky, unwashed man can be a bit of a turn on for me – call me an animal. Not for this boy, however. He wanted me to smell like a bar of soap, fresh and clean all of the time, which, knowing my body, was never going to happen. Also, I didn't want it to. This sort of mocking of my genitals and sexuality continued. We still hadn't had sex and every time we met, he would do the 'penis smell inspection'. De-sexualising me more and more with each encounter, pulling me in and out of the friend zone. I didn't know where I was. He would kiss me almost every time afterwards to reassure me, attempting to assuage my insecurity. 'Oh stop it,' he would say if I looked offended, as though it was a normal thing to do.

But this boy was clearly insecure in himself. He had a clear problem with our height difference, and despite joking often about being a total bottom, would sometimes pretend to fuck me by throwing my legs over my head, all the while saying 'Yeah I'm such a top, fuck yeah!'. However, it didn't stop there. In addition to inspecting my dick, he would pull down my underwear and scrutinise my asshole, similar to a doctor in a clinic. I would throw him off me with a sense of discomfort masked by humour, deep down feeling frustrated and insecure. He would then grab me, hug me, kiss me, and make me feel loved. I thought it was all a game in some way. I allowed this to go on for quite some time. I'm so disassociated with myself at this point in my life that allowing myself to be treated inappropriately like this by men is something almost second nature to me. I somehow try to make sense of their bizarre behaviour; normalise it in a way, so I won't lose them, and won't be left alone again.

We dated for a few weeks. With absolutely no sex. Not one ejaculation between us. One night he even sucked my dick, deep throating me, but it was all a joke. Everything he did was done in jest. He jerked me off while we watched Netflix a few times, but I would never cum.

One day I left his apartment in the morning and did some work at home. He told me he was making dinner for 8:30 and I shouldn't be late. I had a bath and thought it might be a good idea if I jerk off before going to his, then I wouldn't be left with another night of blue balls. I was late to dinner, and he asked why. I told him I'd jerked off. He laughed and said he did too – twice. I felt a rage rush up inside me. I'd only jerked off because I thought he had this weird aversion to any sort of sexual practice, but instead this boy had jerked off twice while I wasn't there. We'd known each other only two weeks and were already finding sexual pleasure separately from each other.

Of course, all of this made sense, when I reflected on it, but instead of pulling the plug and walking out, I stayed. I stayed for dinner, for Netflix, for breakfast, and for another week.

Eventually I came to my senses. I blew my lid one night while I was out, and after a few drinks, I felt completely insecure in myself and the relationship, and could no longer suffer in silence. Thankfully Jägermeister helped release me from its shackles.

I wanted to know what was going on, why he felt the need to desexualise me, and why he was behaving the way he was.

Having dated multiple fuckboys over the past decade, I came to my own conclusion. This guy liked me, but he didn't want to fuck me. He was confused and didn't quite know how to deal with it. Throughout the short-lived relationship, he would proclaim that honesty meant everything to him, but when I started talking about my feelings, he would say it was too much pressure and I was going to give him an anxiety attack. Oh I remember being 22. Saying one thing, meaning another.

I should've known better. I got carried away at the beginning. We spent the first few days together, without taking a break. It was funny, but stupid. I felt free and without any cares. I enjoyed the company.

I wasn't worried about the lack of sex at the beginning. Sex is easy. I was just enjoying the intimacy, the cuddles, and companionship of a man that seemed to like me. But after a while, without sex, it's almost impossible to create a real bond and make it a relationship. It feels somewhat empty and unsure. I wanted all the good things to continue whilst ignoring all the bad. I thought, if I just kept quiet and didn't discuss my issues with the lack of sex, or my issues with the way he treated my body like I was his pet golden retriever, then I could have been happy with him.

This obviously says more about me than it does about him.

In the end, I decided to walk away from things. He talked some nonsense to me about wanting to hangout and not wanting the pressure of a relationship, or labels, or planning on a future. And in between the laughs to myself, I decided it was time to act my age and walk away. I hugged him and said, 'Thanks, it was fun'. He jerked back and said fuck off, in disbelief that I was so casually saying it was over, whatever 'it' was. I said bye and walked home.

He messaged me only a few hours after.

'Do you still want to hang out? I wanna have you around'.

Don't we all wanna have someone around? That's the dream. But we can't just have someone around without accepting the things that come with that person. We can't all just have what we want all the time.

This was a lesson for both of us; unclear intentions are destined to cause somebody pain further down the line●

The 8 Instructions

I'd just moved into my new accommodation after a last-minute extended stay in Berlin. It was the first time I'd been alone in a while, so I sat down and opened Grindr. We all know those kinds of nights. I got chatting to a few guys but, overall, no-one really took my fancy. I was starting to think the evening was going to be a waste, until this one guy started messaging me. No name, no bio, just a cute dark-haired boy, with dark eyes; he was pretty, the boy-next-door-type. We started chatting and he started throwing out some ideas of what he was looking for. I'm pretty open-minded and was excited to hear something different for once in the sea of monotony that is Grindr. Firstly, he said he was into public fun, which turned me on and scared me both at the same time; being in a foreign country and not knowing my boundaries was exciting and terrifying. Breaking the rules and the thrill of potentially being caught stirred in me a dangerous delight. He then described how he enjoyed role play. I've always flirted with the idea of it, but it always made me a bit nervous, like preparing for an audition or a stage performance.

He mentioned a script, which I wasn't keen on. He was a top, and besides being versatile, I was feeling kind of submissive that evening, so I went along with what he wanted. He then came up with a stripper fantasy, in which he was the master who would give me instructions to follow. No speech was allowed, only hand gestures, and he was completely in control.

The exhibitionist in me was completely screaming to come out, so we developed a plan. He wanted to be the only one to gain pleasure out of the encounter, I was simply his play thing – obviously this wouldn't be the case because the whole thing turned me on like gas to a flame – he would cum when he wanted to, and it would be on me. He would then instruct me to leave, covered in his cum: I was to collect my clothes and go. The instructions which would be gestured only by his hand, entirely non-verbal. I had to learn by heart. They were as follows;

1. Take off one piece of clothing.

2. Stretch my body, dance/yoga stretches, etc.

3. Touch and pleasure myself.

4. Dance to the music.

5. Close my eyes for 20 seconds.

6. Smell wherever he points to on his body.

7. Taste wherever he points to on his body.

8. Lay down and get ready for cumshot.

* Extra gestures:
- Hand flat: Slow down.
- Fist: Show ass.
- Thumbs up: Get hard.
- Thumbs down: Get soft.
- Hands together: Time to leave

I got an Uber to his at around midnight. He gave me instructions to his apartment, told me the door would be open and music would be playing ready for 'the show'. I was nervous that I would forget the instructions, I hadn't had long to learn them and they were really fresh in my mind. I kept muddling a few of them in my head. I got to his floor, a little out of breath, nervous and having climbed the stairs. His door was open and so I went inside. I took my coat and shoes off and walked into his lounge. He was fully dressed, sat in a chair, touching himself through his shorts. I stood in front of him. He didn't move for a little bit then he gestured number 4. I felt awkward but that was all part of the act. I danced for him. He gestured number 2. I'd forgotten which one it was so I stood there for a moment trying to recall the instruction. I remembered. I started stretching. I bent over and stretched my arms above my head. Each gesture seemed to last forever. He was taking his time, taking it all in. Taking all of me in. He gestured number 1 and I took my hoody off. I did it slowly incase he'd ask me to slow down. Then he gestured for me to dance and stretch again. He gestured number 1 again, this time I took my top off. I danced again. He pulled his dick out and gestured number 5 so I had to close my eyes. It was frustrating, but it made me so horny. I opened my eyes. Number 7. He pointed to his armpit. I walked forward and as he leaned toward me I licked his armpit. Up and down. It was musky, manly. The smell turned me on. He gestured for me to stretch again. Number 1. I took my bottoms off. Number 3. Finally, I could play with myself. I was so turned on. I rubbed my dick through my underwear whilst watching him do the same. The tension was crazy. He made a fist. I turned around and showed him my ass. Number 2. I bent over forward, stretching so my ass was spread into his face. I stood back up, turned around and he put his thumbs down. I was hard in my underwear, but he didn't want me to be. I stood and looked away from him, concentrating wholeheartedly on trying to go soft. It was so difficult, but it went down a little. Number 1. I took off my socks. Number 1. I took off my underwear. I was now completely naked. Number 2. I stretched in front of him, head between my legs. He was stroking his dick now. Tan, uncut, pink head. Wet and shiny with pre-cum. His dick was fully out of his shorts now and he was slowly jerking. Gliding his hand up and down his dick while looking straight at me. I was rock hard. Number 3. I started jerking off in front of him. He was staring at my dick while sliding his own hand up and down on his own. Thumbs down, and so I faced away from him and concentrated on making myself soft. This time it was trickier, but I focused and turned back around when my dick had gone down a bit. Number 7. He stood up pulled down his shorts and spread his ass, he pointed to his hole. I leaned forward, on my hands and knees and started to rim him. It was even muskier than the armpits. I felt like his slave at this point. I slid my tongue in and out of his ass as he groaned. I secretly played with myself, hoping he wouldn't notice. He turned around and sat back down. Fist. I turned around, got on all fours and showed him my ass. He was jerking off harder and faster now. I could hear his fist beating down on his groin from behind me. Number 2, he gestured. I stood up, bent over and stretched in front of him. He was jerking off frantically and pulling faces like he was edging himself. Number 6. He pointed to his dick. I leant forward and smelled his dick. It turned me on so much. It was a tease to be so close and not put it in my mouth. He made me linger there for a long time. The whole time I was fantasising about taking it in my mouth, imagining what it would taste like. Number 7. I slid his dick in my mouth, it felt soft, wet, and smooth. It slid down my throat so easily, I could tell he was getting close. I sucked his dick, playing with the tip, my tongue doing circles around it while he moaned. He pulled away after a little bit. Fist. I showed him my ass. He continued to jerk off. He moaned while looking at me on all fours from behind. Number 8. My heart raced. He stood up and I flipped onto my back, now lying on the floor. He stood over me, over my chest and beating his hard dick. I saw saliva coming out of his mouth and he spat it onto my face and into my mouth. I was laid on my back, my mouth open, waiting for him to shoot his load. He started to cum. He sprayed his load all over me, my face, chest, it got in mouth and hair. It seemed to never end. He kept squeezing his dick, dripping every last drop on me. Flicking it onto me, off his fingers.

I laid on the floor. He put his hands together. I got up to my feet and walked to find my clothes. I picked them up and walked into his hallway. I could feel the cum still dripping off my beard. I got dressed, smearing most of the cum off my face down my body when I put my t-shirt over my head. I left his apartment and shut the door behind me. I slid my shoes on in the hall and walked down the stairwell with the lights off. I was too horny. After 2 flights of stairs, I looked for CCTV cameras and couldn't see anything. It was dark so I pulled my dick out and jerked really hard. It only took about 10 strokes and I came in the hallway, shooting my load up the wall. I literally exploded. I couldn't wait till I got home to relieve myself of the frustration and excitement I felt.

I left his building and called an Uber. I could smell his ass on my beard and his cum in my moustache. My mind was blown. I've had a lot of sexual experiences, but this had to be one of the hottest. I've remembered those instructions. And next time someone asks me if I have a favourite number, I'll probably say 8 ●

Don't Fall In Love, Sam

He had the sweetest energy. He bounced up the stairs and into my apartment with a big gap-toothed smile. He was around my height, which I liked, and although I'd never met him before, I was excited for the few days ahead. He'd reached out to me on Instagram about a place to stay in Berlin because he wanted to visit. Normally I'd just ignore a message like that, but he seemed innocent, and he was pretty cute from what I saw in his pictures. So, he booked a bus from Copenhagen to Berlin and we decided he would stay with me for 3 nights. Another friend was crashing with me already during this time, so he had to stay in my bed with me, but he said he was fine with that. It made me nervous because I was apprehensive about not getting along with him and then having to share my bed with him for 3 nights. He got to mine quite late on the Thursday evening, we walked to get food and had some drinks. He was tired from travelling, and I didn't really want a big night out. I'd promised myself, if we had any chemistry, I wasn't going to sleep with him on the first night, just in case it was short-lived and then we would have 2 more nights of awkwardness to follow. We went to bed that night, he was very tactile. He cuddled up to me, which I loved, and we talked for a while. We ended up kissing, then kissing turned to fucking, and we ended up having super intimate and passionate sex. We slept – or tried to as much as you can sleeping next to someone you've just met – and then we had sex again in the morning. He was beautiful. Very sweet with an innocence about him that I just ate up. Intelligent too.

The following day he decided to spend it with some friends he had in Berlin, which I was happy about because it gave us some time to breathe. He came home later that afternoon and crawled straight back into bed. I couldn't resist going over to cuddle with him. His energy was magnetic to me.

We left the house and went to see the Festival of Lights. It was beautiful. We had sex again that evening, and it was so close and powerful. I was deep inside him and he held my head close to his.

In the night I got ravaged by mosquitos. It was so bad, that I had to take an antihistamine. As I got up out of bed, I felt a twinge in my dick. I looked down and I saw some white discharge coming from the tip. Great, I thought. I had chlamydia. This beautiful boy had come to stay with me, we'd had sex, and I'd potentially given him chlamydia. I felt awful. I went back to bed. I was lying there, for hours, searching for the right words to tell him when he woke up. As he stirred and opened his eyes, I was rigid, having thought about all the ways I could tell him. 'I've got chlamydia', I said. He asked if I was joking. I obviously wasn't. I told him that I needed to go to the clinic, and it might be best if he got treated too, but it was up to him. That night we were going to a big party, which meant if we got treated that day we wouldn't be able to drink that evening. I was fine with that. I already had symptoms, and didn't want that to get any worse, but he didn't have any symptoms yet, and he decided to wait until he got back to Copenhagen. He came with me to the clinic, we got breakfast, we laughed a little about the situation. He was really calm and understanding about it.

I felt terrible, but he was insistent that it wasn't my fault. I knew this deep down, I just felt awful to have given him an STI as a souvenir on his weekend to Berlin. After I got treated, we went exploring together. He bought me lunch to thank me for letting him stay at mine. I felt awkward allowing him to pay, through guilt about the night before and that morning. We went back to mine after a long day of wandering around, we were both exhausted. I couldn't wait to lay down next to him and he clearly felt the same. He immediately grabbed me and put his head on my chest, holding me tight. It made my heart flutter. I was so content in that moment; I didn't want to go to the party that night. I could have stayed there – frozen in the moment, enjoying his embrace.

I had friends coming over for drinks before the party. We got up and started getting ready. People began to arrive, and shortly after we left to go to the party; but all I really wanted was him. I didn't want to go to the party or be in anyone else's company, I just wanted him. We arrived at the club and undressed to our skimpy outfits that we'd planned. It was a very Berlin party. He looked beautiful. I just wanted him all to myself in bed. We walked around a bit with some friends, and there was a dark and heavy techno room we decided to venture into. He was drinking, so he was having way more fun than I was, but I pretended I was enjoying the music.

It was then, out of nowhere, I felt the feeling of loss sinking in. I knew I was going to lose him. The next day he would go back to Copenhagen and I wouldn't see him ever again. I felt a sharp pain in my heart. I looked across the smoky dance floor, he was dancing. I was two stepping, conscious of my face, trying to mask my sadness. I didn't know why we'd come to the party. We were going to have to say goodbye tomorrow, and instead of spending every precious moment together in bed, we were standing across from each other, separated by random bodies, unable to hear each other over the pounding of the music. I'd just met this boy, and yet I already knew I wanted him to be mine. I felt fucked up. At one point we lost everyone else, he pulled me in close to him and kissed me. My feelings felt validated, even reciprocated. Even in this club full of sexy half-naked men, he still wanted me. My heart pounded.

We passionately kissed and held each other. He turned and said at one point that he didn't want to stay at the party and he wanted to go home. Inside I was elated, but coyly said 'sure, if that's what you want, I don't mind'. We left the club and I called an Uber. I felt sad, but I didn't know why. He reached over and rested his hand on my lap, I held it, but it was limp. He didn't feel fully there. His energy had drifted, and he looked sad. Maybe he was also feeling sad, knowing that this fairytale, whirlwind romance was going to come to an end when he got on that bus home, the next morning. We got home and into bed. I could feel he still had a weird energy, but I lay on top of him and told him how beautiful I thought he was. We kissed and he said, 'I like you, Sam'. I told him I liked him too. We kissed some more, and I leant back, admired him, and told him, again, that he was beautiful. He went quiet. Then looked sad, and whispered, 'But don't fall in love, Sam. We live in different cities'. There it was. There were the doubts and fears I had, properly vocalised. His words pierced my heart. I felt broken. I told him it was fine. I made it seem like I was unbothered, even though deep down I was crushed. I rolled over to my side of the bed and tried to hold back the tears. I couldn't believe how sensitive I was being. His arm was around me, and he was desperately trying to make out with me. I knew I couldn't sleep with him again, he hadn't taken the treatment, this was all going through my head, attempting to distance myself from him through logical thought. But all logic went out the window and I thought, well if I can't love him, then I at least better fuck him good. We then had the most passionate sex I've had in years. He begged me to cum inside him and I did. I was locked into him. I'd lost my head. We fell asleep and the next morning I woke up, sad again. I knew I'd have to say goodbye to him in just a few hours. I was devastated. We held each other tight. We started kissing again, and then we had sex again. There was something about this final time that was even more connected and tangible. It was beautiful. He wanted me to cum inside him again, so I did. We laid together afterwards holding hands, and I suddenly realised he was running late for his bus. He jumped up and quickly started packing. I was feeling super emotional about the whole thing and was trying to distract myself. It was killing me. He got to my apartment door and leant forward and kissed me. 'Bye Sam, thank you so much, I had such a nice weekend,' he said in a sweet voice. We hugged, tightly, and he left down the stairs. 'Come visit me soon in Copenhagen,' he said. I was holding back tears. I went back into the apartment and started to cry. My phone rang. He had forgotten his phone charger.

I wiped away my tears and grabbed it. I ran down the bottom of the stairs, gave it to him, kissed him. 'I miss you already,' I said. He looked into my eyes and said, 'Me too, I miss you already'. He then ran off down the road to catch his bus. I cried●

Copenhagen Boy

His face, held in my hands. Nose to nose.

The warmth I feel, my heart stands still, and my thoughts quieten, for just a moment.

As if nothing exists, just him and I, a breath between us. His smile. Just slight. It's bright and yet it fills me with a stillness.

I can't explain the warmness. The feeling of his skin. The sliding in-between each other, the tenderness of him.

I feel a sense of safety, keys nor locks could ever give. Enveloped in his arms is a reminder why I live.

I brush his hair so gently, an extension of myself. Caressing him is reading me the stories I can tell.

I've been through this before but with him, well he is new. A fresher gaze, a lighter taste, a smile among the few.

He is precious, Copenhagen boy. He's what they say you'll find.

And I promise I'll do everything, to not leave him behind●

Some Days

Some days I think I'm a revolutionary. Some days I think I'm a failure. Some days I think I'm a genius, and some days I think I'm a dunce. Some days I yearn for the stage, while some days I hide in my bed. Some days I wish for stardom, and some days I wish for simplicity. Some days I consider myself a front runner, and some days I consider myself a waster. Some days I am proud of those I love, some days I am jealous. Some days I pour with joy and ease, and some days I leak fear and hate. Some days I don't need to explain myself, some days I answer every unanswered question. Some days I laugh at my missteps, some days I cry. Some days I feel as free as a bird, some days I feel I've clipped my wings. Some days I think I'm perfect as I am, some days I think there's so much to change.

Some days I want more, some days I want to ruin what I have. Some days I'm my own number one fan, some days I send myself death threats. Some days I'm Sam Morris, and some days I'm Sam●

~~Cheating~~

I'm one of those gloomy faces at the airport early this morning. Puffy eyes from crying myself to sleep and having a 4am wake up call. I re-read his WhatsApp messages, over and over. He's so calm and collected, the opposite of how I am. I've been a mess since I found out 2 days ago that he slept with someone else. We'd never discussed exclusivity and having a long-distance relationship, and I guess I knew it was going to be something that came up eventually. I just didn't expect it to come up then. I wasn't innocent either. Three weeks before this, I had also slept with someone else, but it was a blip, and I wasn't proud of it. It happened after a night of heavy drinking and smoking weed, and it was with a friend I used to fuck. I said we weren't to speak about it again and we would pretend it never happened.

I felt ashamed. I flew to see him after this episode and reminded myself that he was important to me. It had only been a week after my visit that he had had sex with someone else. It hadn't just happened by accident. He'd gone out looking for it. This made me feel worse. It made me feel unloved and unwanted, like I wasn't enough. The logical part of my brain kept telling me that sex is sex – it's transactional – but the graphic visual details of him having sex with someone else played over and over in my head like a film reel, stuck on the same scene. It was the first time in my life that I'd flirted with the idea of an open relationship. My therapist advised against the idea, she said I wasn't suited to such a situation, but I wanted to prove her, and myself, wrong. I'm desperate to overcome my jealousy. I knew he cared about me, and that sex is just a need we all have. It didn't take away from what he felt, I told myself. He had told me he felt sad and thought we were both overreacting. He told me he wasn't 'leaving me', and said he hoped that I wasn't leaving him either. But how could I get over this? How could I cope with more of these conversations, more thoughts about him in the arms of someone else, being fucked by some stranger, giving himself over to someone who wasn't me? Maybe it gets easier? Maybe the first time is the hardest to understand, then it becomes routine. I've never been good at sharing anything, especially my boyfriends. I like to feel like they're mine, not anyone else's – they're never up for grabs.

Lucky Escape

Ukulele Chords C E7 Am F

It's such a short love story
I just don't know what's good for me
They always change their mind
And I'm the one left behind
Looking at pictures of you smiling
While I'm at home, alone and crying
I give myself the same advice
That maybe he just wasn't very nice
So, this is what they say
Maybe he's the one that got away
It's a lucky escape they say
Well how comes it doesn't feel that way?

Fearless

$I'm$ so scared. Every day. Every single day I have this fear running through my veins. I wake up and my heart is pounding with anxiety. My blood pumps through my body sending worry into every extremity until I can feel my heartbeat in my fingers. I list off all the things I fear, over and over again. They all take a seat on the chair. One at a time. I replay every worst case scenario. My hands sweating, my mind racing.

"You're so fearless," a friend says to me.

~~Existing~~

I'd been out partying all night, two new friends were visiting Berlin, and during their visit we'd all hooked up. One of them invited me back to his hotel a couple of times, but I politely refused; I didn't feel ready to share a bed with someone. On the last night we went out, I knew there was no escaping going back to his hotel, and so I did. After we had sex, he put his arm around me in bed, and nodded off to sleep, I couldn't hold back the tears. When I realised he'd fallen asleep, I quietly cried to myself in his arms. It felt like a stranger had invaded my space and I was somehow pretending it was him. By him I mean the guy I'd broken up with a couple of weeks before. I'd been looking for distractions, so had drunk more alcohol and taken more drugs in those weeks than all the previous years of my life combined. My highs from MDMA were just about levelling out my extremely dark emotions and only brought me up to a point where I felt more human; while my friends got super high around me, I just felt less depressed for a moment. The comedown was horrendous. The deep, dark depression that followed this moment of liberty was traumatic. I cried hard and fast. I'd be crying so much over the last few weeks that my sternum began to hurt. I had pain radiating across the front of my ribcage from the hunching over, heaving with breathless tears. I felt so helpless and stupid. Break-ups are meant to get easier with time, I should have learnt my lesson by now. I was only seeing this guy for a short while, but for some reason it felt longer. I had invested my time and money, travelling to Copenhagen and back to see him. I had envisioned us together and done all the foolish things someone of my age isn't 'meant to do'. When we decided it wasn't meant to be because of the long distance, it broke me. The feeling of loneliness took every inch of oxygen out of my lungs, it left me feeling exasperated and hollow. I've felt like a shell ever since. I look for distraction in the everyday, but nothing can fill the gap. I partied hard and disappeared into darkrooms. Sex was a way to escape. If a guy showed me any sort of interest or affection my skin crawled. The anonymity and meaninglessness of it all became more of an escape. Sometimes, I hooked up with multiple men in a day. One night I knew I wanted to disappear, I bought an 8 pack of beer, and drank them all one by one at home on my own. I then got dressed and went to a club. I went straight into the darkroom and got fucked by multiple strangers, one after the other. After leaving the club, I cried all the way home, and then cried myself to sleep. My heart was broken, and I didn't know how to fix it. It felt like it was one too many heartbreaks. My therapist wasn't helping, in fact she made me feel worse. Her coldness towards me made me feel even more alone, and like she was just another blocked route preventing me from escaping. Being 30 and having been through so many break-ups already, I wonder if there really is a point. It took me so long for me to open up my heart again after my last heartbreak. It's an uncontrollable feeling. I knew I'd opened up emotionally again this year because I had some romantic interests, one after the other. I felt like I was an attractive, confident, single person, who looked happy and ready to start dating again, and I was. Then only a few months after meeting and falling for someone, he realised he wasn't in love with me and didn't want a relationship. Once again, I was back to the dark and unavailable Sam I was for so many years before.

The sadness has been overwhelming, dear reader, and I'm doing everything I can to escape it; booking holidays, going to the gym, partying, but all it takes is his face to pop into my head and I'm consumed by those dark feelings. I feel like I don't exist again.

Love Is

Love hurts so much but I love love. I love loving things. I love art. I love beauty. I love people. I love love. It's a blessing and a curse. I fall in the hole of love so quickly. I miss the first step, fall down a flight, and slam into a place of illogic and confusion. I suddenly feel the fear of losing the love I've found, more than I do actually feeling the love I've found. I already accept the end of love before I enjoy the love. I await the death of love. The grim reaper creeps behind my shoulder and tells me all of things that will come. My greatest fears. It makes me distrust and worry. I manifest these things, and ultimately my new love starts disintegrating. Piece by piece, I destroy it, with my fear. There will eventually come a time when they will bore of me, and I expect it. I dread it. I don't feel attractive enough, or worthy of love. I love love, but I don't feel like I deserve it. I miss it when I think I have it. I miss love while I love it. I fear love just as much as I love it. Love is beautiful, but love is terrifying.

107

That's Not Me

I cried every day for an entire month. I was fucking exhausted. Thinking about him, thinking about us. Thinking about what could've been. Thinking about what was. Questioning his motives. Questioning mine. Facing the fear that nobody will ever truly love me for me, because I'll never reach the unattainable goal of being the person I've created online. Recalling every person that's ever messaged me online and wondering if they understood that I'm not the product I've created. When he (the recent boy who broke my heart) contacted me online, I thought he was cute and let him into my life for a moment. I stupidly caught feelings and before I knew it, a few months later, I was alone; broken hearted. He came in, got what he wanted, and left. At least that's what it felt like.

Because of what I do, how I make money, how I live my life, people assume I should be treated a certain way. They see me as someone who delivers himself as a piece of meat, to be consumed by everyone who follows me. But this shows they don't get what I'm trying to do. I'm trying to change my industry and the way people look at performers within it. I want sex to be more than transactional; I want the focus to be on the sensuality, love, the passion derived from being entirely consumed by the energy of a person, not simply an exchange of fluids. While I present myself to the world with confidence – personally and physically – I am more than this persona, as most of us are. The digital world we inhabit allows us to be someone else, someone to be looked at, to be seen, heard, experienced, even. But this doesn't mean I am to be treated as an object; I am a person with feelings, insecurities, faults and needs, just like anyone else.

This is probably why, when people meet me they're shocked at my sensitivity and yearning for love. He even said to me that I don't project these sensitivities on my Instagram, so many people won't think I want love because I portray myself as someone who is invincible, self-confident, free, and independent. When really, I'm a lonely guy looking for a place in this world and hoping that someone will love me. The sadness of losing the stability I found in him is both sobering and scary. I'm alone again.

I torture myself with questions about my identity and my work. Will I ever find love being who I am? Should I delete my entire online presence to find romantic happiness in my future? Is it too late? Will I ever know truth again? Or have I sold my soul with no return? I can't face the consequences of this action and I'm devastated by the idea of not having love in my life●

Fiction

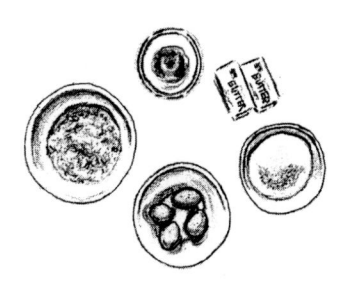

This evening was like looking into a window of someone else's life. I was playing the part of myself, but not committing to being myself. I went with the events, exaggerated my involvement, feigned enthusiasm. I baked homemade blueberry bread during the day and had bought ingredients to cook dinner later. I had cleaned my apartment, top to bottom, and bought new candles. I even bought him a towel, to make him feel more welcome in my home. He was finishing work that evening and then coming straight to my place. I was playing the role of the dedicated house husband, one I'd played before, and the role I've dreamt of playing in the future. In the past I'd experienced it as a fleeting moment (like this one) – it was a dreamscape, a fantasy of an evening with a cute boy I hardly knew. But it had also been a time of enduring frustration and suffocation; feeling trapped with no way out. Tonight was a chance for me to escape. I should know by now that these bipolar moments that I seek in my life of extreme highs in a sea of deep blues, are no good for me, but I'm addicted to the feelings they bring.

He walked through the door, his smiling face made time stop and my heart skipped a beat. The table was set with a bottle of red, and he seemed bowled over. It was the reaction I wanted. Romance. It was everything I wanted in that moment and from a relationship. I was happy.

I felt overwhelmed by my elation. This simple night of romance, dinner and wine, relaxed and comfortable, was something I'd yearned for my whole life. I wanted a boyfriend who would come home to me, who I could cook for, express my love for, adore. I'd become so used to single life. Eating junk food in bed watching Sex & The City on my laptop for the 165th time in a row. I can recite the lines of the show now along with each episode. I think I'm definitely a Carrie, with Miranda's cynicism, Samantha's sex drive, and Charlotte's hopeless approach to romance.

I wanted a taste of this movie romance that seemed to exist in everybody's life but mine, and tonight I was the star of this movie. It was near perfect. We ate, he liked my food. We drank good wine. We talked about everything. We kissed, and mocked each other, we cuddled, and in what had been a moment of darkness in my life, I felt light and innocence. I felt relief.

But my addiction to experiencing both love and despair in equal measures meant this euphoria would soon come to an end. I've spent my life having to say goodbye to things I love. I moved school over and over; I left friends I never saw again when my television or theatre contracts ended as a child. I've spent my life falling in love with things and then losing them almost immediately. Why would tonight be any different? My anxieties about my self image and self-worth make it near impossible to just enjoy the moment for much longer than the moment lasts. I was telling myself to just enjoy the night; make the most of this feeling before he gets bored, or you both realise you're not compatible, or you fuck it up in some way or another. Convincing myself I wasn't good enough or I didn't deserve the happiness I was feeling.

A month before this, I had been lying on the kitchen floor, crying over a guy. He broke my heart. (Or did he? Did I break my own heart? I'm starting to wonder if we get our heart broken by them or by ourselves.) But I was tired of heartbreak. I wanted to just feel safe and happy within that moment. Putting myself in impossible situations, with impossible boys, for the sake of feeling romance, or feeling wanted.

But as I had predicted, the next day, my mood and self-esteem came crashing down like a house of cards. I'd stepped too deeply into a situation I was unsure about, and now I was open and vulnerable to being hurt. I'd let my guard down and shown him the sensitive person I am inside. The exterior had disappeared for a night, and I'd displayed to him who I could be as a partner. I'd opened my gates and let a stranger in, again. It was only a matter of time before I ended up back on the kitchen floor crying.

I had been dating boy after boy after boy until I just collapsed in agony after the last one didn't work out. I felt like I was handing away my feelings, free-of-charge, no commitment necessary.

When do we stop doing this? Does it continue to happen well into our midlife? Or do we just reach a point where we've become bored enough looking for a dream partner, that we give our life up to cleaning up dog shit from the animal that's meant to fill that empty hole in our lives.

I'm not quite sure how I'm meant to fix what is clearly broken in my life. This pattern of allowing people to come into my life and sweep me off my feet, leaving me ungrounded and lost, needs to change, but I've become increasingly disillusioned by love and by people. I feel like it's never going to change. I'm always allowing myself to become someone's shiny new toy rather than their reliable, old faithful. But to allow that to happen, I need to enjoy the journey and not try to get directly to the final product. I need to stop revelling in these one-night wonders of romance and beauty and start to enjoy life in a calmer way. I need to start living in a reality, and not a fiction●

A Friend In Him

Ukulele Chords G Gmaj7 Em C

It's seems like love ain't meant for me
These boys they always leave
I try my best to make them stay
But I can never please
I take red flags with gratitude
Sometimes they even set the mood
I sew them into tablecloths
For which we lay upon our food
I feast upon the hunger
That he drives within my gut
I yearn for him to love me
But I love this fur lined rut
His eyes are looking at me
While I am looking in
The deadness is a killer
And it crawls beneath my skin
It's haunting and familiar
Self-harm is just akin
The unrequited lover
is a friend I found in him●

The bass was palpable, vibrating through my body. Every cell could feel the music. It was absolutely indescribable. I could pick out every percussion and melody. It was running through me. I was hallucinating and dreaming, standing up. I was asleep I think. Occasionally I would open my eyes and I'd moved to another part of the dance floor. I just kept swaying. Losing myself in the music like a zombie. I was entranced. I started tripping into another more enlightened part of my brain. I saw my dead grandmother. She spoke to me and sent her love. I had chills. I cried. My head stared to the ceiling. I evaporated●

A Fig Leaf

The party was forest themed. I had gone as Adam, the first man, and so I was wearing nothing but a fig leaf. I fell to my knees, hysterically sobbing. The tears were uncontrollable and I couldn't catch my breath. Someone I'd met that evening had his hand on my back trying to console me.

'He's here! I told him not to come and he's here,' I cried.

I'd run away from him, upstairs to the backstage area where the other performers and I were storing our belongings. I'd performed that evening in a dance piece that had travelled to Berlin for the night from Prague. I was really excited to perform that evening and it ended up being one of the best runs we'd ever had. After the show I felt pumped and happy.

Earlier that week my Copenhagen boy had told me he was coming to Berlin. He said he was visiting someone for the weekend. In the whole time we were dating he couldn't come to Berlin because he was 'too busy', but now had managed to find time to visit a friend. I felt hurt, I told him to have fun in the city, but mentioned that I was performing at this particular party, and urged him to find another place to go. I wasn't ready to see him yet and I hoped that he would respect that.

I was queuing to get some pictures done with a friend. I'd already been partying for hours now and I thought I'd made a clean run without seeing him.

While in the queue for photos, he walked out. I was face-to-face with him. The last time I had seen him in person, I kissed him in Copenhagen and said, 'I'll see you soon'. My head spun, and I don't remember what I said. He said something, and then walked past me and upstairs. Everything I'd felt for months and months, everything I'd locked away and bottled up, ran through my body.

I ran after him upstairs. He was sat on a bench. 'Why are you here?' I asked him. I was breathless.

'Sam, come on, this party is the main one tonight in Berlin,' he said, defensively.

'WHY ARE YOU HERE?! I ASKED YOU NOT TO COME.' I begged him for an answer.

I was naked but a leaf.

His friend stood next to me laughing and smiling at him. I was humiliating myself. I'd been drinking all night, it was now 6am, and this was exactly the reason I didn't want to bump into him this way.

The whole thing is a blurred mess. I was begging him to tell me why he'd come. I knew it wasn't to see me. And I knew it wasn't out of spite. It was because he truly didn't care about my feelings and just wanted to party, and that was what hurt the most.

Things escalated. I wouldn't let things go. I'd lost my mind. His friends started getting involved, protecting him, trying to take him away from me. He wasn't vulnerable, he was acting like an asshole, but I was alone, and he wasn't.

His friend started screaming at me. 'Asshole. Fuck you, asshole!' she yelled at me.

I left and ran upstairs to put some clothes on. I found my way backstage and fell to my knees. Hysterical. My mind was melting. I was pouring out onto the stone floor. Tears flowing like rivers.

I rushed to put my clothes on. I didn't want to feel exposed anymore.

I sobbed and gasped for air. I was holding my chest. A performer friend was holding my back, trying to calm me down. Nothing could stop me or my heart from imploding.

I got dressed and I went back downstairs. I found him and said I wanted to apologise for getting so angry. I was wiping the tears from my eyes, trying to explain that I wasn't ready to see him, and I thought, hoped even, he would've respected that. I was crying uncontrollably, in front of everyone. It was humiliating. His expression was like stone. I don't remember any warmth from him, any energy he gave me to calm me down or comfort me was absent. He disappeared and his friend tried to console me. I didn't want her around me. She was hugging me saying that he was always like this with guys, and I shouldn't be hurting over him. I said I loved him, she couldn't understand me and everything I said, the words, disappeared into the air without meaning. I looked across the room and saw him with a group of guys. His eyes caught mine. Everything was hazy through the tears. His eyebrows furrowed and he turned his head away. I left his friend and made for the exit. It was daylight outside. 7am.

I walked out and wanted to walk straight into the road.

A part of my heart and soul had broken that night. I crumbled. I made my way home, crawled into bed, and didn't move for 24 hours. I didn't eat, just drank water, and slept. My whole body was a dead weight, I could not lift my body from my bed, or open my eyes.

I'd had a full nervous breakdown and I now had to rebuild my mental and physical health from the ground up.

I shouldn't have allowed him to have this power over me. I shouldn't have allowed him to push me into such a dark space. But seeing him that night was like being confronted with something so dark. It was like I'd seen a ghost. Confronting something I wasn't strong enough for, because instead of respecting my boundaries, he lived for his own.

Our actions have huge effects on others, even when we don't feel them ourselves. Maybe he's selfish for turning up to a place I asked him not to come to, maybe I'm selfish for reacting the way I did, but either way, what ended up being a beautiful night was ruined by an encounter of two people who'd created evil from goodness.

The reaction he triggered in me is something so unforgivable of him or of myself, that I need to remove it, from my universe.

Two ships passing in the night.
Battleships.
Going back to their own waters●

Winter

With the winter approaching and a chill in the air, the memories past are too much to bear.

The sights and the smells that this season will bring, make my eyes open up and my heart start to sing.

The fog in the air in the crisp morning light and the bite in the air on your skin in the night.

The cheap smell of the scarf that you wrap round your neck or the cold of your lips on my cheek when you peck.

The songs that I hear, of good place that they come, just remind me of all the frolics and fun.

I think of the memory that both of us share, the laughter, the learning, the conditional care, but now all the feelings of this time last year, are taken by history and memories dear.

In my soul I would wish for these memories new, but I know that this year they won't be with you.

They say you don't know what you've got till it's gone, and I know what I had so I can't prove them wrong.

I Didn't Say No

I ran down to collect the pizza I ordered on Uber Eats, we hadn't eaten all night having been trapped in the exhibit – we were ravenous. I was pretty exhausted. The exhibition had been open for 3 days already and I'd already had a whirlwind week in New York. I skipped down the front steps of the hotel, when I saw them. Like two lizards creeping into the hotel, slithering their way into the front entrance, grins on their faces and a young boy on their arms. My heart rate quickened, it felt like it was going to burst through my rib cage with a sharp jolt, and I couldn't quite tell whether my blood run cold or hot. My breathing was shortened, as I tried to collect my thoughts and to process what was happening.

They have a house in Miami.
They have a house in Miami.

I had not even thought about it. I was exhibiting at the one gay art fair in Miami, and they had a house here. It was inevitable that they would be here, but the fact had entirely slipped my mind. I grabbed my pizza and swiftly passed them, turning my face away as to not let them see me. As hard as I might have tried, I couldn't avoid them completely. My name was all over the exhibit and we were bound to run into each other at some point in the evening.

As quickly as I could, I returned to my exhibit room (which was also my hotel room) and dropped the pizza. My friend was talking to me, but the words vanished in the thick haze of panic which had come over me.

'I ... I can't believe who I've just seen arrive here...' I spluttered out.

I could barely find words and I couldn't process what I was meant to do about the situation. 'What? Who is here?' my friend asked, confused. I looked panicked and flustered. 'It's a long story, I didn't think they would be here, I haven't even thought about them since.... I completely forgot they had a house here. They have a house in Miami, and in fire island, but they live in New York. I remember they invited me to their house in Miami once. I completely forgot they...'

I didn't even know where to start. This was something I'd chosen, in a sense, to forget about, to move on from. I had left it behind, and here it was, arriving at my art exhibit. I stopped, my whole body still, and tried to explain to my friend why I was reacting this way. We were hiding in the back of the exhibit. I needed to tell someone.

Years ago I used to go to a house on Fire Island as a house guest. These two men ('them') would host a lot of boys there, for free; we would simply stay there and enjoy the island. There was nothing untoward at the beginning, contrary to what you might think, and I had some amazing summers there. Until 2 and a half years ago. I arrived on the island, and the frenzy of steroid pumped, cis, white men who littered the island didn't phaze me anymore. The wild deer wandering the island were spectacular and a complete contrast to the madness of the partying and the falseness of the people who spent their summers there. That being said, there is a beauty in the hedonism that is freely expressed on the island. It's a place where you can be gay without being judged. That's probably one of the only things that you won't be judged for.

I'm an INFP-T on my Myers-Briggs type. I'm a bit of an introvert and often misunderstood in social situations, which can be difficult when you hop from party to party, introducing yourself to cardboard cutouts, one after the other; there's always the fear that you'll literally vomit if you have to say the words 'Hi, nice to meet you' one more time.

My friend Frank and I arrived at the house. He was a tall and individual looking guy, not the usual Fire Island kind of man. He always looked out for me while I was in New York, and so he was a great person to have around while on the island. You always need someone around you that you can trust while you're there. We went down to our room and put our bags there. I wanted to sunbathe almost immediately. I'm typically British, so deprived of sunlight that when I get the chance to bronze-up, I will jump at it. I grabbed my towel, put my speedos on and went out the garden to lay on a sun lounger. When we went out into the garden, we were greeted by the other house guests. There was a bubbly, very chatty, girl, Mariana; a fairly quiet taller gentleman, Alessio; and then a shorter, Latin-looking guy with a beard, Sebastiao. He got up from his sun lounger and walked toward us to introduce himself. I couldn't help but notice his dick bulging in his speedos. The veins were protruding through the thin yellow fabric, and it was quite clear he had fluffed himself moments before to make himself appear bigger. Occasionally I would catch eyes with Frank, it was one of those moments you have with friends; you don't need words, just a look to acknowledge that something funny was going down. He started passing around a joint. I smoke weed, but not too much, and I didn't want to get too fucked up before the day had even begun. Frank took a few drags and then Sebastiao brought the joint to me. He sat on my sun lounger and passed it to me. It was being passed around, but for some reason he felt the need to bring it all the way over to me himself. I took a drag, and then looked over at Frank. One look to suggest, this guy is really trying it with me, and we have literally only just walked in the door. Frank totally got it. Everyone took a few more drags, and then Sebastiao came over to me, again, to offer me the blunt. I declined. He seemed confused but walked back to his sunbed.

After a little while I turned to Frank and mentioned that I wanted to take off my speedos. I really didn't want tan lines on my ass. I was shooting a bunch in New York and had worked hard leading up to the summer to get rid of them. He told me just do it, so I did. I slipped my speedos off, in a very discreet way, and laid on my front. I didn't feel embarrassed, and I was as discreet as I could be about getting completely naked in front of a bunch of mostly strangers.

Later that day we were all headed to drink and dance a little before dinner took place at 10pm. We ventured down to the dock, where the bar was, and it was like Grindr had haemorrhaged all over the bay. Frank and I really just wanted to watch Drag Race, so we decided to forfeit this party and walk to Cherry Grove.

'You're leaving this party to go and watch television?' Sebastiao complained.

'Yes. We are' Frank and I both said at the same time, while laughing with one another.

We parted ways with the group and headed to watch some television. It was a lot of fun, and we were both very happy with our solid choice to leave the party. We headed back to the house to make it back in time for dinner at 10pm. Dinner at the house was always a serious affair. Laid table. 3 courses. A lot of wine.

The two older men who owned the house were now here. I always felt a bit nervous around them. I guess we were staying in their house, so I always felt like I owed them something, or like I should be on my best behaviour. You know when you used to go around your friend's house, when you were a child, and then you'd have dinner with their family, and you'd always feel somewhat uncomfortable? That's what I felt like in this house on Fire Island every time I visited.

There was the usual dinner party chit chat, people laughing at things that weren't funny just to keep the mood elevated. People talking about how 'exquisite' the food was. This food was certainly not as exquisite nor sublime as people kept insisting.

I was sat next to Alessio, a seemingly conservative character: Italian, living in New York, about to enrol on a

Master's course at Columbia University. He was insufferably boring, but there was something about him that was charming, and underwhelmingly sexy, which was quite refreshing on the island. He asked me what I did for work, which I always find a startling question, particularly at a dinner party. I began to explain about social media, Instagram, and how I made my sole income from a website I ran to which my fans subscribed. You'd think I was pitching for investment, but it was simple dinner party chatter. He had no idea what I was talking about and became more and more judgmental and rude. Smirking to himself and mocking everything that came out of my mouth. I didn't want people to overhear his interrogations into what it is that I do with my life, so I simply said,

'Look, we're from two different worlds, you don't have to understand what I do. It's fine. We're only existing in each other's lives for one weekend, let's make it as sufferable as possible'.

He hardly understood what I said by the looks of it, and it was at that point I realised he seemed quite drunk. He proceeded to get up, wine glass in hand, and headed toward the kitchen to get more wine. The next thing I heard was the smash of the glass wall he had just walked through, shattering it to a million tiny pieces. He stopped in his tracks. The whole table turned and gasped, and he stumbled back. He proclaimed to everyone that he was fine, while pulling inch-long shards of glass out of his hand. Blood was now dripping everywhere and there was a mild hysteria growing among everyone. Some were running to find bandages, some were running to find towels to mop up the blood, and the rest were consoling Alessio and his bleeding hand. I also went over to inspect his hand. I thought it would need stitches, the cuts were deep, but everyone insisted he could just bandage them up and the wounds would heal by themselves. And so, they did.

Alessio was embarrassed, and when I was alone with him again, he told me how stupid he felt, and that he was concerned he would no longer be remembered on the island as the tall, handsome, Italian man, but as the Italian man who walked into a glass door. I agreed with him, and solidified in his mind that, yes, he would indeed be remembered as the guy who walked into the glass door.

After he was bandaged up, we all started getting ready to go to the underwear party in Cherry Grove. By this point we were all fairly drunk and were seemingly ready to go to a club where you check your clothes at the door.

After moments within arriving I lost Frank. I assumed he'd gone to the dark room at the back, and so I didn't go looking for him. I wandered around for a bit. Got a few drinks, and then I found Alessio and Sebastiao. Alessio seemed to have got over the embarrassment of his recent misfortune, and decided to ask me about what it was I did again. I couldn't tell whether this was his way of flirting or not or just winding me up. Either way, I decided to show him my Instagram. I thought it would be easier than trying to explain. He took one look at it and said, 'Do you ever want to get married?'

I was fairly taken aback. I mean, I didn't want to get married this weekend, but maybe someday.

'Well, not right now, no. Why?' I said to him.

Through a gargled laugh he said, 'You will never get married'. I fell silent. I sort of couldn't believe he'd said it, but then I also know that's what a lot of people think when they see my Instagram, so, this was not new territory for me.

'Thats a pretty awful thing to say to someone,' I said to him. He was laughing, and after a few seconds could tell he'd offended me. He apologised, and even though I could tell it wasn't sincere, I accepted it anyway, as I didn't want to ruin the night.

After this rather uncomfortable exchange and feeling rather annoyed by it all, his friend Sebastiao was suddenly by my side. He had some poppers which he was thrusting under my nose. I didn't mind. I inhaled and within a fraction of a moment my head was spinning. Alessio did some, too. We both flung our heads around to meet each other and immediately started kissing. I don't know why I'm such a sadomasochist when it comes to men, but the meaner they are to me, the more I'm interested. Not enjoying the kiss, I pulled off Alessio, and then Sebastiao started dancing on me. He was very handsy, and he pushed his face closer to mine. I was drunk, and fairly delirious on poppers by this point, but I still wasn't really interested in getting together with him. He was grinding on me, and I could feel that his dick was hard in his pants. I really wasn't interested, so kept pulling back slightly, and trying to head back to Alessio.

By this point in the night, there was still no sign of Frank – he had my phone and my wallet, as I didn't have any pockets so I'd given him the responsibility of looking after them for me. I wanted to go home, so I suggested we look for Frank and then head out. After hunting through the dark room, like someone who'd dropped their sunglasses in a pool, I finally found him.

We all made our way back to the house to get into the hot tub. There's nothing better than sliding into a hot tub after a whole night of drinking.

We all took our clothes off and slid in. There was me, Frank, Alessio, Sebastiao, a friend they'd picked up called Michael, and Mariana who'd woken up from her sleep to join us. Someone had rolled a joint and started passing it around. I smoked some and it hit me pretty hard. This was some strong weed. Normally I don't have such a lucid trip from smoking weed, but when I laid back in the hot tub, I was counting the light reflections of the water up on the trees, in almost a frame per second view. It was extremely bizarre. As I looked across the tub, I could see Sebastiao playing with himself under the water. I averted my eyes back to the trees. Somehow that was more calming.

In a moment of alcohol and marijuana induced madness, we all decided to go down to the beach, completely naked. It was one of those fun, only-on-Fire-Island type experiences. We left the house and headed down to the beach. It was so liberating, all of us, completely naked, just walking down the beach front at dawn. Alessio was the last to get completely naked. He had shorts on, but he was soon peer-pressured into taking them off. The sun was rising, and it was a really beautiful morning. It was about 7am at this point, and we walked the entire stretch of The Pines beach, and then back up onto the boardwalks. As we were walking back to the house we walked past many people getting their morning coffees, wishing us a good morning, while we would cover ourselves with our hands occasionally just out of respect, although these people have pretty much seen it all on this island, so it didn't matter either way.

When we got back to the house, I ran to the outdoor shower to wash a lot of the sand off me which I'd collected while on the beach. A joint started doing the rounds again, and so I took a few drags and then headed downstairs to bed. Alessio wanted to join me, and I was fine with it. I knew nothing sexual was going to go down as we were so wasted. By now it was around 8am and all we wanted to do was go to sleep.

We got into bed together, I snuggled up beside him, and we started nodding off. The door to our room creaked open and Sebastiao came in and got on the bed. He started asking if we were horny and wanted to get up to some fun. Alessio and I didn't even get up to anything and we were already in bed together, so the idea of a threesome was definitely off the cards. Sebastiao then proceeded to play with himself, and eventually pull his erect penis out in front of us both.

'Come onnn... It'll be fun... let's play' he said, while jerking off over the top of us.

Alessio was uncomfortably giggling, as this was one of his close friends. I was just trying to ignore it so he would go away. Alessio told him we weren't interested, but Sebastiao wasn't content with this answer and kept begging for us to play with him. I said I was going to sleep. We were so drunk, and so high, and so tired by this point that now our heads were on the pillow, we just wanted rest. He seemed to eventually surrender and leave the room, I'm not sure at which point this happened as I had started to fall asleep. Within seconds I was out like a light.

During my sleep I remember hearing the door creak open, again. I felt a body sliding under the covers behind me. I was asleep, holding Alessio, on my side, I then I felt something behind me, pushing between my legs. I vividly remember feeling something slide inside me. It was very slow, and wet. It wasn't painful, but I was confused as to what was happening. The feeling was somewhat of an enjoyable physical memory in my body, but my subconscious mind was telling me that this was wrong. I froze in bed. I then remember that behind me went still, everything went still, and Alessio got out of the bed and left me alone with him in the bedroom. In that short moment, I was fucked hard and fast. I was startled into consciousness and realised that Sebastiao was now raping me. It got harder and faster, and then he pulled out. I heard him breathe heavily, groan, and then get up and leave the room. I lay there in shock. Time had gone into reverse, sharply and quickly. I didn't know what to think about what had just happened. I didn't fully understand what had just happened. Someone had got into my bed while I was sound asleep, had sex with me, unprotected, finished himself off and then left. I reached my fingers around to feel my ass. There wasn't any cum, so I assumed that when he quickly pulled out it was because he came on himself, either that or deep inside. I didn't know what to think. I hadn't said no, but I also hadn't asked for it. Alessio came back into the room and got back into bed with me. I was so confused and shocked that I couldn't process exactly what had just happened. I went back to sleep holding onto Alessio and said to myself that I would figure it all out the next day when I woke up.

I woke up the following afternoon and went to the bathroom. I stood in front of the basin and looked in the mirror. I looked tired. I saw on the counter a bottle of Truvada. The label read the name Sebastiao. I breathed a small inane sigh of relief. It was a small amount of comfort in a moment of confusion.

I went upstairs to breakfast, and most people were already up, drinking champagne, and having coffee. I felt a bit delirious. I said good morning to the older hosts and went out into the garden.

Sebastiao was there. I didn't want to look at him. His face somehow distorted and unpleasant to me. He walked over to me. 'Morning! How are you feeling?' he said to me quietly.

'I'm ok, just tired' I replied.

I was trying to brush off conversation with him.

'Hey, listen, do you remember us having sex last night?' he said to me.

I was taken off guard and didn't know how to respond. I looked around me and rubbed my eyes to hide my embarrassment.

'It's just, I felt like I might have been raping you, but then I wasn't sure whether you were just into the rape fantasy or not, so I was a bit confused'.

I was startled and lost for words.

'Oh, yeh, no, its fine, don't worry about it,' I mumbled.

I didn't know what to say, and I barely had an explanation to myself of what happened last night, let alone to him. I felt very confused and uncomfortable.

'I need some water,' I said and walked away from him.

I saw Frank and asked him if he'd leave the house and go for a walk with me down to the dock to get some coffee. He obliged and I started to tell him about what had happened.

'So, I'm not sure, but I think I was raped last night,' I said, in my usual matter of fact, dry way of saying things.

His face was still for a second and then he started asking a bunch of questions. He was pretty horrified when I gave him the answers. He knew that Sebastiao had been in pursuit of me from the moment I'd arrived, so he'd seen the progression of this happening as a bystander. He was furious and started explaining to me that without consent, it's rape.

'But I never said no,' I said to him, 'I just laid there unconscious and let it happen'.

This was what confused me the most. I just laid there, and let it happen to me. I didn't speak up. I didn't stop it. I didn't defend myself. I just let him fuck me. I let it happen.

Anyway, after this had happened, I left it. I spoke to my friends, Frank, etc, and let it go.

Frank took it upon himself to bring it up back at the house. I never asked him to, he just felt angry and that it needed to be addressed. He mentioned it to the girl friend who was also staying there that weekend, and chillingly she was unsurprised by Sebastiao's behaviour. However, word got back to the owners of the house, and they had a different opinion. At this point it's worth noting that they are both lawyers, as is Sebastiao, and they are all friends.

Frank was uninvited to the house with immediate effect, and so was I. They told him that we were no longer welcome, and that the issue was to never be spoken about again.

One of the owners emailed my friend in a rage saying that I was making it up, and that it never happened. He never spoke to me once or asked me what had happened, he was totally covering for his friend without any questioning whatsoever. I took it upon myself to email the owner of the house myself because I was so angry that they were taking it out on my friend. It had nothing to do with him, and ultimately it was my business. I sent him a very lengthy email with a detailed account of the events of that night, similar to what I've done here, to which he replied: 'Sam: I do not wish to respond or comment'.

Well he's a lawyer after all.

And so there I was. Almost 3 years later, at my art exhibit in Miami, and the two men who owned the house that this happened to me in, who had uninvited me and shunned me out, silenced me and my friend, had just arrived. I now had to face them, and ultimately a trauma that I had buried, whilst smiling to other attendees and fans.

I took a bite of my pizza and hid. I felt my body shaking and I didn't want to be there. I lost my appetite and I started drinking.

I drank and drank but couldn't get drunk.

Instead I felt more and more mentally unwell, and I couldn't face anyone anymore. People were coming into my exhibit and I was ignoring them. I couldn't focus.

I saw the couple walk past my exhibition, notice my name on the door and keep walking. They were laughing. It chilled me and I couldn't stay open any longer. I closed my exhibit early.

I received a tweet from a disgruntled fan saying that I didn't pay attention to people and that I was rude. It hurt me but I didn't have the energy to address it. This was way bigger than that evening. There'd been no justice, just silence and repression. The only way I would win in this circumstance was to become stronger in the face of these two twisted perverts, and continue to grow and inspire others to reign over the ownership of their bodies.

But to share with you a weaker side of me, that night I closed the doors of my exhibit, took all the bedding from my bed and slept on the floor of the walk-in wardrobe of my hotel room. I was vulnerable. I wanted to hide away and disappear until it all went away.

The next day I got up and carried on as if nothing had happened. One day I'm sure I'll have to address all this properly, but until then I will write it all down as a form of therapy, and continue to make empowered work, celebrating sex, self-empowerment, and most importantly, consent●

Mine

The valleys and the waterfalls
The rivers and the lakes
The rough parts and the smooth parts
And the filling in the cakes.
I lick my lips and feel the surface
The imperfections over
For bits of me will drop & fall
And I will never own her.
I touch myself. It's soft to touch
My stomach and my sides
But moist and musky does become
The warmth between my thighs.
Take off the armour, show the pink
The wetness and the silver drink.
The smell envelopes, thoughts & things.

Familiarity is teaching me
To taste the smell to test my brain
And linger while im there.
I softly hold the warm inside
And play with all the hair.
A temple with a field to play
A meadow and the sun.
I'm free to roam the streets of me
Through the beige I run.
The flaws I find will govern me
In my love and in my art
But never overwhelming me
Enough to sell my heart.
I love you perfect wonder
Of the world in simple form
There's nothing I would change
As with a rose must come a thorn.
So here I love and cherish
The body I will own
Until the day I leave it
And it lays upon a throne●

Circle of Stones

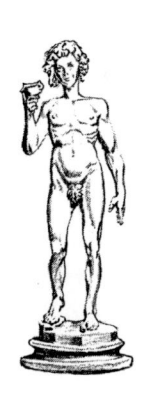

As I mooched through the Athens tourist trap gift shops like a foreign stray, not differentiating myself much from the stray cats in the area, I felt hungry, lonely, and displaced. Finding food in a foreign city is an anxiety inducing sport for me. I usually fill the need for food with iced coffees, always locating the nearest Starbucks upon arrival, but once the caffeine and sugar crash makes me dizzy, I usually have to find solids. Travelling alone makes this more of a stressful event, I don't want to sit in a restaurant by myself, but equally I can't just live off fast food alone. I get some souvlaki. It's delicious, hits the spot, and I didn't feel too anxious ordering and eating.

I pick up a handful of different Greek god figurines. They were cheap, pretty, and I thought they'll look cute in my apartment. Maybe tacky, but who cares. It's been 5 days since I've had any real human contact. No one has spoken to me, or called me, in almost a week, and the sense of loneliness is both daunting and familiar. I start to feel jaded. Every city I travel to starts to feel the same. It's just me, again, in a different surrounding. No one to share it with, no one to even talk to about it after. It's just me. I start to question life as I walk through the ancient ruins of Agora. How pointless it all is. Life. Civilisations and monuments, gods and temples, all reduced to rubble with a €4 entry fee to walk around and take useless selfies. I stand in the ruins of an entrance to an old theatre. Huge towering columns adorned with gods & monsters. I take pictures I'll never look at again, and then I move out of the way of the woman behind me, so she can take pictures she'll never look at again. I sat down to sketch. I wasn't sure why I was sketching or what for, but I did it anyway. What would my place have been in Ancient Greece?

Probably more purposeful than my place now. I imagine I would've been a vital cog in a system that needed hands and brains to grow. And where am I now? Contributing very derivative work, alongside many, many other 'artists' doing the same. I'm not a cog, I'm decoration. Human decoration. Civilisation doesn't need any more waste. Human waste, wasteful art and opinions; waste of space. The Greek gods gave us so many individual explanations and examples. Then they were all reduced to one. One God to rule us all. Easier. Brain condensing. Keep it simple, for the minions. I'm rambling. Thoughts chasing thoughts down paths in my mind.

I'm ready to go home now. To maybe find purpose in a simpler setting. Let gods be gods, and let humans walk and feel the ground beneath them. Recently I lost my ground. I'm floating. Not a god, not a human. I'm in a nowhere land, just existing, a dormant life. I try to find purpose, and birth joy from creation; but then I fear I'm driven not by art, but by the yearning to be remembered after death, like these towering marble columns still standing above the dirt and rubble. Why? I ask myself. For when I die, so will my ego. Why is my ego fearing my death more than I? It's like my body will turn to dirt, but my ego will stand like gods & monsters. Well, a monster it certainly is. A monster that needs to be fed. Well maybe I'm running out of food. Maybe I can't feed it any longer. I don't want to hunt for any more options of how to feed it, so maybe it's time to simply let it die. Let my life be a circle of stones in the ground that tourists will pay €4 to unknowingly walk over for millennia to come.

with love, Sam

THIS BOOK WAS FINISHED IN 2020

Sam Morris ©
www.sammorris.me